# TREAT YOUR MAN LIKE A DOG...
# AND LIVE HAPPILY EVER AFTER

*A relationship primer for women who love dogs*

## Maïa Madden

Treat Your Man Like A Dog...
And Live Happily Ever After

ISBN: 978-1-935125-26-6

*Photographs by Alicia Dickerson*
*www.fourleggedphoto.com*

Book printed in the United States of America

To order additional copies of this book go to:
**www.RP-Author.com/Madden**

**Robertson Publishing**
59 N. Santa Cruz Avenue, Suite B
Los Gatos, California 95030 USA
(888) 354-5957 • www.RobertsonPublishing.com

# CONTENTS

# FOREWORD

by

Fred Luskin, Ph.D.

Author of *Forgive for Love*

W hat relationship would not benefit from more forgiveness and understanding? Who is not capable of changing their attitudes from critical and mean to accepting and kind, if they really want to? In *Treat Your Man Like A Dog...And Live Happily Ever After*, Maïa Madden asks women who love dogs to observe how caring, admiring, accepting, forgiving, understanding, playful, honest and kind they are with their dogs. Then, with a smile and a gentle nudge, she urges women to extend their dog-loving ways to their mates if they want their relationships to endure and thrive.

As director of the Stanford University Forgiveness Project in Palo Alto, California, I have spent more than ten years researching the healing power of forgiveness. I teach couples a practical seven-step process of forgiving that enables them to overcome their differences and communicate lovingly. Forgiveness is crucial to the survival of relationships, but first must come a willingness to recognize that negative attitudes, past resentments, critical words and harsh judgments stifle long-lasting love. Using humor and anecdotes, *Treat Your Man Like A Dog...And Live Happily Ever After* helps women initiate that first step by realizing that the way they treat their beloved pets is much kinder and more thoughtful than the way they often treat their mates.

Whimsical yet empowering, *Treat Your Man Like A Dog... And Live Happily Ever After* never scolds or insults women. Instead, it illustrates how unconditional love is an attainable goal, one they already share with their dogs. It is a wake-up call for meaningful change, with instructions included.

Just as women choose their dogs, they choose their significant others, for better or for worse. Once they commit to their choice, they do not expect a Yorkie to act like a Saint Bernard, yet they think it is possible to control and change their partners. This book tells women that they can only change themselves, and urges them to focus on loving their mates for who they are, not who they expect them to be.

*Treat Your Man Like A Dog...And Live Happily Ever After* asks women to be grateful for their men and show it with praise and affection, just as they do with their dogs. Instead of harping on what men do wrong and dwelling on past offenses, women can choose to see the good in their husbands and lovers and learn to rejoice in the present moment, as dogs themselves do. Once they take responsibility for changing themselves and realize how blessed they are to be loved, they will be ready to implement the seven steps to forgiving, which I have seen work miracles in faltering relationships. Women who love their dogs will get a head start by reading this book and taking its lessons to heart.

Fred Luskin, Ph.D.
Author of *Forgive for Love*

# PREFACE

*"You cannot do a kindness too soon
because you never know
how soon it will be too late."*
Ralph Waldo Emerson

One morning, I was complaining about the dirty dishes and my children's messiness and the unfairness of being expected to do everything for everyone. As I was heaping buckets of surliness and resentment on my hapless boyfriend, who was trying to read his newspaper in peace, my beloved Pug-a-Poo, Rocky, scampered into the kitchen. Interrupting my tirade, I bent over to pet him and tell him what a good boy he was and ask him if he needed a walk, all in the sweetest voice imaginable. My boyfriend looked up and said, "Rocky is the only one you are always nice to."

This silenced me like a stab in the heart. I couldn't stop thinking about it. I felt ashamed that I didn't show the same feelings for my loved ones as I did for my dog. I started thinking about my friends who were so attentive to their dogs and yet often so nasty and dismissive to their partners. What if we could treat our mates as well as we treat our dogs? Wouldn't we all be a lot happier?

In an article in *Vanity Fair* magazine, the designer Oscar de la Renta, when asked what he would like to be in his next life, replied, "A dog, so my wife would love me more." How pathetic that such a talented, intelligent man felt he didn't get the love he needed.

And how sad that so many men feel the same way. How many women praise their dogs but never their men? How many women stop whatever they are doing to pet their dogs, give them treats and profess their undying love while completely ignoring their husbands? How many women tell their friends stories about how sweet and smart and loyal their dogs are, yet share only complaints about their relationships?

I started observing women with dogs in the park, on the street, at outdoor restaurants — even at the hairdresser's. Sure enough, almost all of them, especially the over-40s, treated their dogs with utmost solicitude and respect. Not so their husbands, if they still had them. There, I saw neglect and dismissal, at least when the women didn't know I was spying on them. The same held true for many of my friends. I had never noticed how much they took their mates for granted and how unkind they could be at the slightest provocation. Their love spigots turned on and off depending on whether they were dealing with their dogs or their partners.

Now, by suggesting that women treat their men as well as they treat their dogs, I don't mean to suggest that men *are* dogs. (That comparison is often taken as an insult, although in my book it is the highest compliment.) Men are a little more complicated, but all in all they are much simpler than women. Like dogs, they have certain needs and characteristics that women can easily grasp and just as easily satisfy in the same loving way they do with their dogs—if they choose to.

Maybe you are murmuring to yourself, "I certainly don't love my dog more than my husband." That may be true in the abstract, but is it true in real time? Are you blind to how you act? Do you need a wake-up call before you end up with just the dog? Take my little quiz in the first chapter and try to observe yourself as a stranger would. Then think, "Who feels more loved by me, my man or my dog? Who seems happier? Whom do I embrace without reservations?" Be honest.

It's never too late to be kind. It's never too late to be grateful for the people and pets in your life. And it's never too late to change your ways, especially by practicing love in the here and now, where it counts. The first step is to take a hard look at yourself and your relationship and watch your thoughts and actions as if you were watching a movie. Compare those thoughts and actions with those you have for your dog. The lesson is *that* obvious. Once you start changing how you think about your man and how you act toward him, love and appreciation will replace indifference and scorn, and you'll both be much happier.

So many mushy books tell us what dogs can teach us about life but fail to mention the most important lesson of all: that the way dog lovers treat their pets should be the way they treat each other: with concern, kindness, affection, acceptance, attention, honesty and playfulness.

Therefore, without any wish to offend, I will sometimes call men dogs in this book — that is, dogs we love and pamper and want to be with. Dogs we feed and pet and buy bones for, even if we are vegetarians. If you don't love your dog, don't bother to read this. If you do, it will make perfect sense.

# DO YOU LOVE YOUR MAN ENOUGH?
## TAKE THE TEST

In order to determine how much you need this book, please answer the following questions. And be honest…

1. With whom would you rather sleep?
   a. *Your partner*
   b. *Your dog*
   c. *Your man next to you and your dog in a doggie bed or on your bed, if that's what both of you like*

2. It's Sunday morning and your mate is getting frisky, do you:
   a. *Stay in bed and have some fun?*
   b. *Jump up and go for a jog with your dog?*
   c. *Have some fun and then all go for a jog ?*

3. You get a second dog and insist that she also share the bed, even though your partner objects. Who ends up in another bed?
   a. *Your man*
   b. *Your dogs*
   c. *You would never insist!*

4. It's a beautiful weekend morning. What do you do?
   a. *Fill the cooler and head to the beach with your mate*

    b.    *Take the dog to the beach alone and hang out with other dog lovers*

    c.    *Plan a great day at the beach for all of you*

5. Your dog is circling you for dinner and your man is asking you what's for dinner. Whom do you answer in a sweet voice and oblige immediately?

    a.    *Your partner*

    b.    *Your dog*

    c.    *Both if possible*

6. You come home tired after work, and your dog and your partner are there when you open the door. Who gets hugs and kisses and cheery hellos first?

    a.    *Your mate*

    b.    *Your dog*

    c.    *Both*

7. If you are busy and your dog comes up to lick your hand, then your man comes up to give you a hug, to whom do you respond with a loving touch and kind words?

    a.    *Your man*

    b.    *Your dog*

    c.    *Both*

8. You have a little extra money, so you want to splurge. Do you:

    a.    *Reserve a romantic room for two for Valentine's Day?*

b. *Buy your dog a designer leash, a fancy new bed and lots of toys?*

c. *Plan a romantic weekend and find someone to watch your dog?*

9. Your husband asks you to go on a trip with him. Do you:
    a. *Say yes right away*
    b. *Say you have to stay home with the dog*
    c. *Say you will call the dog sitter tonight*

10. With whom do you spend more leisure time?
    a. *Your partner*
    b. *Your dog*
    c. *Both in different ways*

11. Your dog has a tick and your man has a splinter. Who gets your help?
    a. *Your man*
    b. *Your dog*
    c. *First your man, then your dog*

12. Whose picture is on your cell phone?
    a. *Your partner's*
    b. *Your dog's*
    c. *The picture changes regularly*

13. Whose picture do you have in your wallet?
    a. *Your mate's*
    b. *Your dog's*
    c. *Both, among others*

14. Your dog goes out to do his business and your husband goes out to get the newspaper. After an hour, neither is back. Who are you worried about?

    a.  *Your partner*
    b.  *Your dog*
    c.  *Both of them or neither – they're big boys*

15. You cooked a huge steak for dinner. Your man would love a steak sandwich for lunch tomorrow, but your dog would love to eat the rest right now. What do you do?

    a.  *Save the steak for tomorrow*
    b.  *Cut it all up for the dog*
    c.  *Give the dog the bone and some tidbits and save the rest for a sandwich*

16. To whom do you say "I love you" the most?

    a.  *Your partner*
    b.  *Your dog*
    c.  *Both of them, of course*

If you have ten or more **b** answers, you MUST read this book.

If you have twelve or more **a** answers, you need to have a talk with your dog.

If you have twelve or more **c** answers, you are doing something right but read the book anyway!

## WHO'S THE BEST DOG?

*"This is the miracle that happens every time to those who really love: the more they give, the more they possess."*
Rainer Maria Rilke

A woman sits at an outdoor table with her Cocker Spaniel at her feet and her husband next to her. She is constantly leaning over to pet the dog and offer little treats. Not once does she touch her husband's hand, look into his eyes or speak to him, except to complain that the mocha she is drinking is the worst she's ever had.

I have a good friend who confessed that she said "I love you" to her dog many times a day, but had never been able to say it to her husband without feeling embarrassed. She's English, but that can't be the whole story.

No wonder so many men say they don't feel loved in their relationships. Yet even if a woman says "I love you" at all the right times, she often fails to show her love in the little ways that mean so much more.

## Pet me, please...

If we gave men half the petting and kissing and sweet talk we give our dogs, they would be happy indeed. Men need and deserve at least as much love and affection as our dogs do, if not more. A good back rub is a good back rub no matter who you are.

When Lynn's dog, Rowdy, a big, black, dread-locked Puli she adores, comes up to her and nuzzles her hand, she stops whatever she is doing to pet him. If he rolls over on his back, she rubs his tummy and tells him he's her baby. God forbid her partner interrupt her when she is at the computer or on the phone. She admits he would get a scowl, not a smile or a hug or even a peck on the cheek.

My sister lies down on the floor to rub her brown Labrador's tummy while he thumps his tail and licks her face. Her husband looks on wistfully. "Why does Toby get all the affection?" he asks. She tells him not to be silly.

If you don't believe physical touch makes a huge difference, even though scientists are proving that it lowers blood pressure, improves health, accelerates healing and ensures long-lasting romance, try a little experiment. For one week, pretend your man is a dog you love. Touch him gently whenever possible. Kiss him. Make eye contact and hold his hand. Massage his shoulders if he's tired. Rest your hand on his leg. Speak to him in an affectionate way instead of curtly or sarcastically. Make his favorite food (unless he's a dog-cook, a rare breed indeed) and sit close to him at dinner. Your pretend dog will soon be as cuddly, friendly and devoted as your real dog. And soon you won't be pretending at all.

We love our dogs for their constant devotion, but if we ignored them, scolded them and scorned them the way we often do our men, that devotion would disappear. We cannot take devotion for granted; we must earn it and deserve it.

I witnessed a glaring example of disrespect in the supermarket. A middle-aged woman surveying the tea selection tells her husband to find her a decent tea. He asks what kind she would like. "Never mind," she sighs in the most exasperated voice. "Go get the guy who helped us last time. He'll know what I want." In one instant she has bossed him, scolded him and made him feel useless and stupid. And for what? His devotion in the face of such blatant dismissal of his worth is senseless.

## What a good dog!

A dog-loving woman will praise her pet when he does the smallest thing: come when called, bring back the Frisbee, sit and roll over or simply put his head on her lap when he senses she is sad. She will talk to him in a sweet voice and give him a treat to let him know how pleased she is.

Do we give this kind of praise to our husbands and boyfriends? Rarely. Do we appreciate what they do for us? Maybe we do, but we don't often show it.

Just as a dog wants to please his master, a man wants to please the woman he loves. Yet we fail to give praise, let alone treats, for all the big and little things our men do for us. After a while, they no longer want to do anything for us because they don't feel appreciated. Not feeling appreciated goes both ways, of course, but what you give is usually what you get.

I remember one Saturday when I came home to find that my then-husband had rented a rug shampooer and steam-cleaned all the carpets. Then I saw that he had also steam-cleaned the pillows and sofas, leaving everything wet and, in my imagination, ruined forever. Instead of thanking him for his hard work, I went ballistic and accused him of destroying my precious pillows. They turned out to be just fine. It was I who had ruined something much more precious: an opportunity to be grateful and loving to a man who was trying to please me.

An ignored dog is a sad, frustrated dog. The same goes for a man. By criticizing instead of praising, you are saying that he is not good enough for you. How would you feel if your man were constantly commenting on the inadequacy of your hair, your clothing, your cooking, your intelligence or your work? You would probably defend yourself with a torrent of words, or leave. Men don't respond with a torrent of words, but they do leave.

Nicky is in the process of getting a divorce. One morning, she was shocked to hear her once-cherished husband say, "You are so beautiful. I love you." Those were the words and the tone he had used when they were first married, but now he was talking to the dog. Perhaps her insistence that Duchess sleep on their bed and he sleep in another room if he chose to (which he eventually did) had a wee bit to do with his leaving the marriage.

We don't expect our dogs to bring us flowers or jewelry to show us they care—a lick will do just fine. If we learned to be thankful, instead of always wanting something more or different, our mates would be as happy to be with us as our dogs are, and just as loving.

Make it a habit to praise your partner for his good qualities and loving deeds as they occur, and he will want to do even more for you. "Thank you for doing the dishes." "You are so thoughtful." "The lawn looks great!" He will feel happier about doing chores and respond with the same kind of loving attention to what you do for him. Instead of creating a negative atmosphere, you will bring harmony into your home.

## Please don't get mad at me

I have seldom seen a dog-loving woman scold her pet for more than a minute, and then only if he has done something naughty in her presence, such as pee on the rug. Even then, she will stay as calm as possible and bring the dog outside in order to change its behavior, not punish it. (If you hit your dog, get out of my book!)

Nor do most women nag their dogs. "When are you going to stop licking your butt?" "Isn't it time you got out of that chair and did something?" "You make such a mess when you eat!"

Any woman who thinks that rubbing her dog's nose in his poop is a good training technique is nuts. Her anger and the violence of that act, especially if she didn't witness the offense, will only make her dog cower and run away. But if a man does something wrong, many a woman will think it's fine to rub his nose in his mistake over and over again. No wonder he runs to the garage or out the door.

What woman in her right mind would bring up a dog's past offenses? "Remember the time you chewed up my best shoes? I still can't forgive you for it." "See that spot on the rug. That's where you decided to throw up. It's ruined forever." "I am still so angry that you scratched up the door to the kitchen."

Yet a woman rarely forgets a man's transgressions, even when they occurred a ridiculously long time ago. She will bring them up again and again and again. Surprise, girls: after a while, your man-dog doesn't hear you; he doesn't understand why you are rehashing his mistakes; and sometimes he doesn't even remember the event you're talking about. Like a dog, he lives in the present and loves in the present.

Sometimes a man is so inured to hearing himself criticized for a past mistake that he will assume you are about to re-criticize him, even when you aren't. For instance, my ex had a crazy, grudge-filled mother who would bring up the fact that when he was a teen he had thrown out a plastic mimosa plant without her permission. Now, this woman was such a hoarder that her young sons had to move into an adjacent hotel room when her piles of shoes, perfumes, hats, magazines, liqueurs, cans and boxes threatened to bury them alive during the night. Yet her son's one attempt to clean out the closet was met not with gratitude but with life-long anger that grew increasingly virulent as she aged…and made him dislike her even more.

Don't spoil the happiness you can have today by bringing up the past and recycling bad energy. You will hurt yourself as much as you hurt your man.

## Sit! Stay! Off!

You train your dog with rewards, not threats and entreaties. Likewise, it is much easier to train your man-dog with gentleness than with constant nagging. How ridiculous would it be to beg your dog to sit and scream at him if he didn't? Or whine at him when he didn't come when called?

Let's say you want your husband to pick up his clothes or take out the garbage or put the toilet seat down. Proper training is all it takes, and that means catching him when he does something right, not yelling at him when he does something wrong. When he takes out the garbage unbidden, tell him how much that helps you and say thank you. Reward him with a kiss. When he puts his dirty clothes in the hamper, notice right away and give him a hug. Like a happy dog, he will be doing what you like in no time.

The trick is to continue the praise even after the training has been successful. Consistency is key. You wouldn't stop rewarding your dog once he learned how to sit and stay because he would soon forget or not bother to listen.

And even though you should be consistent in rewarding and thanking, you don't want him to take it for granted. Be random with your rewards to keep him on his toes. It might be a "thank-you" one day, a kiss another and something altogether spectacular (in his book) another. If a dog thinks that he might hit the jackpot of a big beefy bone, he will be much more likely to perform consistently in anticipation of more than a scratch behind the ears. Just think what a man will do for what he wants most…

You shouldn't stop being grateful and thankful for all the things your man does for you, even if you've been together a long, long time. And you shouldn't forget to reward him either, whether it's with a little treat or the whole enchilada.

# I CAN'T HELP IT, I'M A DOG

---

*"Let me be a little kinder*
*Let me be a little blinder*
*To the faults of those around me*
*Let me praise a little more"*
Edgar Albert Guest

Dogs like to sniff each other's butts. They like to eat grass and roll in mud. They leave paw prints on the rug and hair on the bed. Some drool. Some snore. They knock vases over with their tails. If given half a chance, they steal food off the table or counter. They gnaw on dirty bones and hide them behind the sofa pillows. They dig holes in the garden. They bring us dead birds and expect praise. Yet we try to change them only if their behavior is harmful. Otherwise, we love everything about them because they are OUR dogs.

Why will a woman so readily accept her dog's idiosyncrasies and not her man's? The minute she feels secure in a man's love for her, she starts trying to change him. Soon she is showing little respect for who he is as a man and an individual, and he resents it.

## Dogs will be dogs

A woman complains to her friends that her husband wears scruffy old t-shirts all weekend. She forgets that he wore scruffy old t-shirts when she fell in love with him, and it didn't bother her one bit back then. Instead of nagging him, she could go out and buy him some nicer t-shirts. Eventually, he might notice them and try them on. Or not.

If a husband loves watching thrillers, his wife will drag him to chick flicks. If he prefers football and beer, she will reserve theatre tickets and dinner at a fancy restaurant. She will try to change his manners, his speech, his hobbies, his friends and his food. She will drag him to a big city when he likes camping. In short, she will make him feel inadequate and unloved while depriving him of the things that make him happy.

My French grandfather was a fisherman, a hunter, a gardener, a musician and a loner. My grandmother was a refined lady who loved to shop, travel and socialize, who couldn't sing or dance, and who stayed indoors to protect her perfect white skin. When she realized she could not change him, she decided to let him be and still do what she liked. She went to Paris with girlfriends, traveled alone to see her family in the United States, and lunched and shopped in the city at least once a week. (He, on the other hand, loved everything about her and never once tried to change her.)

If your man is so bad, why did you choose him in the first place? You don't get a Rottweiler and expect it to act like a Miniature Poodle. If you choose a German Shepherd, do you try to turn it into a Chihuahua? We spend time studying the breeds we like before we buy them, and some of us are perfectly content with a loving mutt.

You knew what you were getting in your man, at least you should have known, so trying to change him later is selfish and offensive. His self-esteem will plummet with every effort you make to transform him into your idea of perfection.

Okay, I'll admit there are some bad dogs that no one, except maybe the dog whisperer, can handle. Perhaps they had traumatic puppyhoods. Perhaps they had mean owners who turned them into mean dogs. Perhaps they were bred to be aggressive and nature trumped nurture. Keeping them is pointless.

If your man is violent, abusive or addicted, by all means get rid of him. But if he is what he is, a good man you profess to love, let him be. And if you just can't love him the way he is, let him find someone new who can and will.

Of course, there is also the argument that some men want to be coddled and improved, that they lack the confidence and ability to choose clothes for themselves or decorate their apartments alone. These men are grateful for a woman's help. In fact, they often ask for help and are relieved to have the burden of making such decisions lifted from them.

Your man may very well be like that, in which case you are not manipulating or coercing him to change. You are merely allowing him to express himself with the help of an expert, namely you. This is akin to hiring an interior decorator to give you the resources and choices you need to express yourself successfully. Or finding the perfect sales associate to bring you clothes she or he knows will flatter you most.

My man can't be bothered to shop for himself. That doesn't mean he resents my buying him nice shirts, especially when the compliments roll in. He knows he looks better, thanks to me, and that not only makes him feel good but also saves him time he could be spending on the tennis court.

For the sake of comparison, let's use grooming our adored dogs. Bathing them, brushing them or fussing over them doesn't mean we don't love them the way they are. It just means we love them even more when they smell good and look great.

## Woof! Woof!

When asked to describe their perfect man, women will often use words that describe another woman: sensitive, communicative, emotionally available. They don't expect their dogs to act like their best girlfriends, but they do expect their men to, even though it's impossible. Instead of appreciating masculine traits, they demand that their men display feminine behavior, and then complain when years of emasculation destroy the strength and confidence that attracted them in the first place.

Most men talk when they have something to say, not to fill the void. Unlike many women, they don't find hidden meanings and emotional implications in every comment, and they are frustrated when you do. They tend to be more stoical and shy away from talking about their feelings.

That doesn't mean they have no feelings. Because men don't emote the way we do, we have the audacity to think they don't feel pain, frustration, sadness, loss, insecurity, loneliness or boredom. We don't ask our dogs to emote so we can know how they feel. A simple woof will do.

"Why are you so sad?" we ask the Bloodhound with the droopy eyes. He may not be sad at all, but we immediately try to make things better with a treat, a cuddle, a game or a walk.

If we realized how hard it is for many men to verbalize their feelings, perhaps we would be as sensitive to them as we are to our dogs and not demand the instant feedback we expect from our female friends. Perhaps we would respond with a hug or a kiss or just some down time, instead of attacking them with a barrage of questions and accusations. It is sometimes wiser to let things be than to insist on explanations.

"Richard looks so uncomfortable when I ask him questions about our relationship," says longtime girlfriend Rachel. "Instead of answering, he looks away, mumbles something and finds the quickest escape route."

Rachel has learned not to ask the kind of questions that make her man shut down in fear and confusion. Instead, she waits for his nonverbal cues of love and relies on his initiating an intimate conversation when he feels relaxed and safe. That way, instead of a head-on collision of emotions, she gets a gentle exchange of true feelings. It may not have as many reassuring words as she would like, but it does have the sincerity and connection she craves.

## My dog makes me happy

What probably depresses a man most is feeling that nothing he does pleases his woman. He'll keep trying and trying to find the right words and do the right things until, eventually, he gives up in frustration. He won't tell her how he feels lest she pooh-pooh him or tell him it's his fault for not "listening." She doesn't even notice he is defeated, because she's usually too busy venting her own frustrations.

But with her dog, it's a different story. She spreads joy all around him when she takes him for a walk, gives him a treat and tells him he's the best dog in the world. He spreads joy all around her because he is loved.

If you spread joy instead of anger, your man will love and value you even more than your dog does.

Try to notice how your partner feels by his body language, not by an irritating third degree interrogation that he will meet with more silence. Then be as nice to him as you would be to your dog, by paying attention to him and showing love through what you do, not through what you say.

For instance, my dog-park friend Shelley admits that in the evening after work all she wants to do is put up her feet and enjoy a glass of wine. Yet here comes Clancy, her Irish Setter, whining at the door and looking at her with those enormous Setter eyes. His body language is VERY clear. She doesn't ask him if he wants to go for a walk, why he wants to go so badly when he has a huge yard to play in, or why he can't see that she is (dog) tired and needs to relax. No, she gets the leash and heads out, rewarded by leaps and licks and a wildly wagging tail.

Fast-forward four hours and here comes Jim, her husband, bringing her a bowl of Cherry Garcia ice cream, snuggling up to her on the sofa and massaging her tired feet. His body language should be very clear to her, but she chooses to ignore it and falls asleep without giving him so much as a peck on the cheek.

And what about gratefulness? Have we forgotten how to be grateful? Especially if a man is supporting his wife and children, showing gratitude is the easiest reward to give. You are grateful to your dog for his companionship and love, yet dismissive of the many things your man does for you. Men often say that their women take them for granted. Instead of feeling like heroes and being rewarded with love for their hard work and loyalty, they live in silent misery wondering what they have done to deserve such scorn.

No matter how much time Marty spends working in the yard, fixing up the house or making sure Linda's car is in perfect condition, all she cares about is whether he puts his dishes in the dishwasher. Everything is subsumed by that one symbol of helpfulness, and all her resentment is attached to that breakfast bowl making it out of the sink ASAP. She is blind to Marty's enormous contributions to the home and complains endlessly about how the dishes pile up waiting for her to do them.

Linda might take a lesson from her dog here. He doesn't put his dish in the dishwasher either. It's just not what he does. But he sure does a lot of other things right as he tries to please her and love her in his incomparable doggy fashion. And she is ever so grateful. Marty wishes he were that lucky.

## Love him unconditionally

I saw a newspaper photograph of the winner of the world's ugliest dog contest. He was bald, scrawny and half-blind. The owner, a woman, said he was the sweetest, smartest, best dog she had ever owned. That he was ugly only made him more lovable.

Every dog has its lovable traits, even if no one else notices them but you. And every dog has its shortcomings, too, whether it's chewing up shoes, barking too much or jumping up on visitors. Yet we love our dogs despite their faults. And they love us as if we had none.

How amazing relationships would be if we loved our mates unconditionally and accepted their idiosyncrasies without criticism or complaint. "Let me be the person my dog thinks I am," goes an old saying. How about, "Let me love my man as unconditionally as I love my dog." Dogs teach us so much in their unwavering, enthusiastic affection. We can learn even more by watching how we pour love, affection and attention on our adored dogs without effort or obligation. Our men deserve at least as much, if not much more.

If love is the highest virtue, then giving and receiving unconditional love is the ultimate reward. It doesn't matter if your dog-man is short, tall, fat, skinny, bald, a nerd or a jock. It doesn't matter why you love him, just that you do. It doesn't matter what others think of your love, only what you think.

Pretend your man is the most lovable dog on earth, and treat him that way. Better yet, don't pretend. Believe it.

Love and friendship are essential to a good relationship, as is forgiveness. From animal rescue stories, we know that most so-called "bad" dogs, with the exception of those who attack without provocation, can be reformed through love, patience and training. We don't give up on our dogs when they have problems or behave badly; we accept that they have lovable traits as well as faults. Women should not give up on their relationships just because there are setbacks and discouraging moments. You forgive your dog when he jumps on you with muddy paws. You forgive him when he runs into the street, destroys your flowerbed or steals the rest of the chicken. Why is it so easy to forgive your dog and so hard to forgive your man?

It is sometimes said that only dogs love unconditionally. Not true. Their unconditional love for us releases ours for them and makes us better humans. To love your man the way you love your dog means giving unwavering, unconditional love for who he is, not who you wish he would be.

Just as your relationship with your dog evolves with him through many stages, from puppy to frisky adolescent to wise adult to old soul, your relationship with your mate goes through predictable stages of love and commitment. It is interesting to note how many women can only go through the first few stages before they lose their love and loyalty. The minute the going gets even a little tough, they start toying with the idea of a new relationship and make less and less effort to salvage the love they have. The same can be said for men, of course. Many men and women then start again with a new partner only to arrive at the same stumbling block with the same excuses and resentments and the same lack of desire to overcome obstacles and preserve the relationship.

These very same women would be appalled if you suggested they turn in their dogs for newer models if their dogs got sick or were maimed in accidents or were disliked by their best friends. "What kind of person would reject an innocent animal when it needed your help most?" they would ask. These are the kind of women who rush to adopt Hurricane Katrina rescue dogs yet have never ventured into the local pound.

If your dog were hit by a car and needed emergency surgery, would you hesitate to pay for his care and not pray that he would survive and be with you for a long, long time? Or would you think, "I'll just get a new puppy and not waste my time and money?"

Unconditional love means through thick and thin, sickness and health, struggle and wealth, good times and bad times. It means fidelity and the willingness to save a relationship when the going gets rough. It means remembering what is worth saving and keeping love sacred even when life tests you again and again. It means having faith that your relationship will succeed, and doing everything you can to achieve that goal even when it seems defeat is everywhere. It means asking for love to prevail and believing with all your heart that it will if you sincerely and completely and unequivocally want it to.

## DON'T IGNORE HIM OR HE WILL STRAY

---

*"Too often we underestimate the power of a touch, a smile, a kind word, a listening ear, an honest compliment, or the smallest act of caring, all of which have the potential to turn a life around."*
Leo Buscaglia

D o you really love taking your dog for a walk early in the morning when the rain is like an icy whip on your cheeks? Or at night, after a long day of work, when flopping down on the couch is your only desire? Do you resent feeding your dog once or twice a day and making sure he has clean water? These are must-dos for dog owners, and most women perform them willingly and without complaint because they understand and respect their dogs' needs.

And what about their wants? We take our dogs to the dog park for an hour when we could be reading a good book or watching a movie. We hike with them and bike with them and run with them, and we learn to enjoy that time, even if we didn't at first, because we love them and want them to be happy.

Like dogs, men are easy to please. Their needs and wants may vary, but they are not hard to figure out. Luckily, men, unlike dogs, are not totally dependent on us for everything. A man can fulfill most of his wants himself. But wouldn't it be nice if you sat down with him and relaxed after work instead of jumping up immediately to start dinner or help the kids with their homework?

Instead of greeting your man with a distracted peck on the cheek and rapid-fire griping about your day, try giving him real attention. If you stop to think that HIS day may have been rotten too, you will let him unwind feeling loved and appreciated, instead of ignored and unnecessary. After all, when your dog jumps all over you when he first sees you, you don't push him away and tell him how tired you are. You pet him, talk to him, play with him and tell him how much you love him and miss him when you're apart.

Barbara never hesitates to get down to her Maltese's level when she comes through the door, even if her panty hose snags as she puts down the grocery bags. Giddy is just such a cute dog; she's worth it. Barbara hurries to put away the perishables, change her clothes and grab the leash to take that sweet Giddy for an evening romp. How ashamed she was when she realized that if she came home and her husband opened the door, she would brush right past him and into the kitchen to feed Giddy and start dinner. No hugging, no kissing, no romping, no animated greeting — nothing for the most important person in her life.

How do we let ourselves act this way? What amnesia makes us forget to show affection to those we profess to love while showering our pets with the time and effort we claim not to have for our men?

## Be with him as much as you can

Most women I know spend a lot of time with their children, their friends and their dogs and hardly any time alone with their mates. Men may not want to go shopping, but perhaps they love taking care of their yards. Would it be so hard to join them now and then? It is in the quiet side-by-side moments that intimacy grows.

When we first pair up, we spend every minute with our beloveds, getting to know them and cherish them and make them happy. Then, as the years go by, the closeness we nurtured begins to dissolve. Much too soon, two strangers are living parallel lives without each other's love and support because they failed to maintain their bond of intimacy. What a waste.

Now think about your dog. Do you stop petting him, walking him, caring for him and playing with him just because you've had him for a while? As he gets older, do you go about your business as if he didn't exist? Do you show him less and less love and abandon the rituals and routines you once enjoyed? Not if you're a true dog lover. In fact, your devotion and attention grow the longer you have been together.

How easy it would be to show the man you profess to love the same attention. Instead of growing apart, you would deepen your love with each passing day.

I am not suggesting that you give up your own pursuits for a man's sake, or that you insist on sharing all his hobbies. You don't forgo lunch with your friends for your dog. You don't decline a vacation because you're afraid to leave your dog. You don't ignore your own needs to fulfill your dog's needs unless you are truly neurotic. And you seldom hesitate to leave your dog alone when you need to work or attend to your affairs.

But day in and day out, you spend at least some time looking after your dog, keeping him company and doing the things he needs and loves to do. You do it consistently; it is part of your life, not an arbitrary decision. ("I feel like walking my dog today—he's been cooped up for a week.")

My friend Janet had a German Shepherd mix she loved. When we were in college, Sharetha lived in our dorm room and slept on her bed. Janet picked the college, she said, because they allowed dogs (these were the hippie years). The dog went wherever we did, and Janet spent hours at the beach running and playing frisbee with her best friend. A few years after graduation, she noticed Sharetha struggling to get up and running ever more slowly and painfully. It turned out she had degenerative hip dysplasia. Janet did everything she could to make her dog's life as good as it could be and continued to dote on her until Sharetha died.

If you want to have a great relationship, give the same kind of steadfast, loving attention to your man as you do to your dog. A dog that is not fed, not petted, not cuddled, not entertained and not cared for will soon stray. So will any man.

## Which brings us to sex...

Sex is to a man what petting is to a dog: essential. A woman will use all her sexual powers to entrance a man, then after she's captured one, it's bye-bye sex. At least it is according to many men (and many honest women).

"I can't be bothered," says one of my friends. This as she sits on the sofa petting her dog while her husband walks around like a miserable prisoner. Does she think "I can't be bothered" when her dog nuzzles her for a good scratching behind the ears? Of course she doesn't.

I once saw a man reach out to hold his wife around the waist at a concert. She pulled away as if a leper had touched her. When her dog licked her hand, she immediately leaned over to pet him.

If women realized that many men bond through sex, that they need sex to be happy, that sex is their way of showing love, they would think twice before saying "I'm just too tired tonight."

Men have feelings too, but most women see only their own because men tend to suffer in silence — until they can't take it any more and leave.

We don't need our dogs to talk to us and beg for attention. We give them our affection freely and without manipulation. "Do you need to cuddle?" "Are you sad?" "Did you miss me?" We spend more time trying to figure out our dogs than we do our partners.

Even when our men's nonverbal cues are perfectly clear, we will often choose to ignore them. Later, our excuse is, "Well, he should have said something. I'm not a mind reader."

In reality, women are mind readers. It's men who are not. Beware the wrath of a woman if her man doesn't intuit what she wants, when she wants it and how she wants it. The double standard is blatantly unfair to men. Women, who are so often superior at communication, have the nerve to brand their men as poor lovers because they fail the female guessing games. Women will turn off their talking skills, then complain that their men are not meeting their needs, then go on to shut themselves off sexually because "he just doesn't get it." Wow, no guy stands a chance of winning that game. It would be akin to withholding verbal cues from your dog when it's time for a walk, then expecting him to fetch his leash and scratch the door, then deciding that he might as well go pee in the back yard if he isn't excited about going for a walk.

The truth is that there would be two losers in that scenario and a missed opportunity to exchange love and caring and create more love and caring in the future. The loss for a couple is even greater because, unlike a dog who greets each day with renewed hope and excitement, a man will slowly stop trying to entice and romance you until his desire for you wanes and dies—and your lack of desire for him turns you into a cold semblance of the woman he once loved.

Women will complain that their men's sexual needs are unreasonable, selfish and annoying. Therefore, women should not be forced to "give in" when they just don't feel like it. Do you regard your dog's constant need for love and attention as unreasonable and insensitive to your feelings? No, it makes you feel loved, and you are happy to reciprocate. In fact, the very act of giving makes you feel better.

I know a woman who just got another dog, even though she works full-time and has children. Her marriage lacks affection and intimacy, so she lavishes all her love on the dogs. She doesn't have time for her husband, but she has plenty of time for the dogs. As a result, he, too, gives and gets his love from the dogs, and the occasional lover.

How hard can it be to change your attitude about sex? Just do it. The more you have, the more you'll want, and your man will love you as much as your dog does. If you're sincere and persistent, you will rediscover the joy and attraction you once felt for your partner.

Perhaps you can take a cue from your dog here. You know how you develop rituals with your dog, such as going to the same dog park at the same time every afternoon and giving him a bone every morning when you take off for work? If rituals create lasting bonds with your dog, why not develop rituals with your mate, ones that reinforce your connection and trust on a daily basis? Making a ritual of sex and romance can only make your relationship stronger. No dog, and no man, will run away when he knows good times are always on the agenda.

## Be spontaneous and generous with love

One of the things I have noticed about my dog-loving friends and myself is that we ALWAYS respond when a dog approaches us for attention, even if it isn't ours. Our reactions are pure and spontaneous. We say something sweet, scratch behind their ears, give them a little treat or let them sit with us as we gently pet their heads and necks.

Sadly, another observation I have made is how rigid and unresponsive we can be when our men come up to ask us a question or just be with us. We rarely respond with a spontaneous kiss, a quick hug or a gentle inquiry. Rather, we either ignore them completely or ask, ungraciously for the most part, "What do you want?"

Okay, I am exaggerating a little here, but if you make your own informal survey you will see what I'm talking about. What is spontaneous is often what is real, what comes from the heart, not the head. No thought or ulterior motive interferes when we respond to our dogs; an expression of love and happiness arises instantly from the good part of our being, the part still connected to universal love. If that part is so easily triggered, why do we turn if off to our men? Are we embarrassed? Blocked? Unhappy? Resentful?

Whatever the reason, it is just that: a bad, self-destructive reason. And reason has nothing to do with love. To cultivate the kind of pure reaction you have to your dog and spontaneously lavish it upon your man whenever and wherever he comes near you, you must tell your mind to shut up and let your heart take over. That means practice, practice and more practice: the same kind of practice necessary for meditation or present-moment awareness. It means immediately replacing a bad thought with a good feeling and letting your body respond accordingly. Perhaps you have a cherished memory of the two of you in blissful accord. Keep it ready to blip on your mental radar whenever you need it so you can respond to your husband with affection and concern, then and there.

Perhaps it is simplistic to believe that good feelings and positive thoughts will generate more of their kind and come back to us without limit, but if we look at our love for our dogs, we see how true this concept really is. The bliss we feel when we are with our treasured pets is surely a cosmic refraction of the positive love energy we send them day after day, moment after moment, beyond all reason and conscious effort. Wouldn't it be great to harness that same energy in our relationships by shifting the way we love?

# LET HIM PLAY

*"All work and no play makes Jack a dull boy."*
James Howell

Why does he need all those old cars? Why does he play golf every Sunday morning instead of being with me? Why does he buy so many tools when he hardly ever uses them? How can he sit through two football games drinking beer and shouting with his buddies? Why does he spend money on new cameras, new computers, new televisions, new mobile phones and any new gadget that catches his eye?

Listen to any group of women talking about their men, and the magnitude of their griping will astound you. But if they are talking about their dogs, it's a different story.

## Toys and buddies are essential

"Sara loves her plush toys. I buy her a different one every week."

"Have you been to the new dog park? Georgie goes crazy playing with the other dogs. I take him there for an hour every day after work."

"We keep a big basket full of toys in the apartment, that way the dogs never get bored."

Dogs need their toys, and we gladly oblige them. Men need their toys too, and we glee-fully deride them. We fail to buy them the gifts they want, choosing instead the gifts we want them to have, such as ties and shirts.

When men buy their own toys and spend time playing with them—whether they are amplifiers, electric drills, tennis rackets or golf clubs—we resent them for it. We rejoice when our dogs love their tennis balls or squeaky toys, yet we complain when our men love their motorcycles or HD televisions.

Something is wrong with this picture. If you love your man, you should want him to be happy and fulfilled. If a man feels that he has to sneak away to do the things he likes to do, he will start seeing you as the Great Dictator. "Got to head home or the old lady will kill me."

Little boys love to play games, alone or with each other. They need to. So do grown men, but women often think that's ridiculous.

They think men should spend all their time with the family.

Have you ever watched a bored man being dragged around a store by his chatty wife? I always think how much happier he would be playing ball with his friends, hanging out at home or tinkering in the garage. She would be happier shopping with a woman who shared her enthusiasm, yet there they are, two unhappy people pretending to have fun.

All dog trainers stress the importance of "socialization." They want us to make sure our dogs play with other dogs as often as possible so they don't become aggressive or timid. We take them to the park, and we socialize as well. We are pleased to be good owners. But when our men want to go out and play, we complain or pout or guilt-trip them into staying with us instead.

We become like bad dog owners, selfish, unloving women who don't respect men's needs. Always let your man play with other dogs (oops, I mean men) if you want him to be socialized and happy.

My friend Annabel thinks it's absolutely mandatory to take her dog, Max, for a walk in San Francisco's Marina district all the way along the beach to the Golden Gate Bridge. She does this every Saturday morning, rain or shine, and has developed a regular coterie of dog-owning friends.

Annabel's husband, Ian, is Irish and wants more than anything to join a rugby team that practices during the week and plays games on Sunday mornings. You would think she would encourage him and be happy that he wants to stay fit and "play" in a "pack" of men with similar interests. After all, Max loves to play with his Saturday pack of dog friends.

You would think. But Annabel is dead set against Ian's rugby dream. After all, Sunday is their "special day."

Would she consider changing her Saturday schedule to accommodate her husband's wishes? Of course not! She can't deprive Max just to please Ian, and she can't imagine changing her walk to Sundays because that's not the day Max's best friends show up.

## Bring me the ball

A dog-loving woman will throw a ball over and over again to her pooch if he loves to fetch, but will balk if her husband asks her to accompany him to the putting green or the tennis court. She has plenty of time to amuse her dog but none to play with her man.

Most women have skewed priority lists: children, dogs, friends, parents, jobs, homes, oh, and mates. The men usually come last when they should come first for relationships to thrive. No wonder so many men feel unwanted and invisible in their own homes.

Put your man at the top of the list and share at least as much time with him as you do with your dog.

When we got divorced, my ex-husband complained that I would never sit down and watch an entire football game with him. Instead, I felt duty-bound to cook and clean, to take the kids to the park and, of course, to walk the dog. I had forgotten how to play. (On the other hand, perhaps he had forgotten how to appreciate what I did to make his football watching possible, but that's another story.)

When we first get together, we play all the time. We walk on the beach, picnic in the park, go to the movies and watch late-night television; we ski or skate or hike or take road trips together; we wrestle and tickle and laugh. We have fun. Then, gradually, the fun dwindles and life gets predictable and much too serious.

Your dog brings you a rope and you play tug of war. He brings you a ball and you play catch. You don't turn away with a sour look and a complaint. Even if you're pressed for time, you take a minute to amuse your dog and make him happy.

Ask yourself, "Am I spending more time with my dog than my partner?" If the answer is yes, make your man the top dog and give him equal or greater time.

That can be hard for a woman to do, given her need to multi-task and her urge to do it all. Lynn was on the brink of divorce when she decided to find time for Jeremy. Instead of devoting all her free time to cooking for the week ahead, getting caught up on paperwork, reading frantically for her book club meeting, taking the dog for long walks and volunteering for every school fund-raiser, she resolved to take a full hour every day, no matter what, just to be with Jeremy. It didn't have to be for a serious talk or dinner at a restaurant or a planned outing. It could be watching a show together or sitting side-by-side reading the newspaper. Anything to be close. She had the kids walk the dog after school, bought pre-roasted chickens and vegetables for dinner, taught the children how to make their own lunches and do their own laundry, and learned to say "no" to excessive volunteering. She quit the book club, the PTA and the church choir and never brought work home from the office. Miracle of miracles, the home, family and job did not collapse, and neither did her marriage.

## Don't keep him on a tight leash

Have you ever watched a dog on a very short leash walking at his master's side? He cannot sniff anything, stop anywhere, or greet another dog because his collar is pulled tight around his neck like a noose. Like a tie around a man's neck on a hot day.

This dog is not having fun, although his discipline is admirable. A good owner makes sure her pet gets plenty of time off leash. You let your dog run around like crazy at least once a week, yet you expect your man to be tame and housebound even on the weekend, after five days of being tethered to his job. What a mistake.

The freedom to run and play and be wild is essential. When your dog comes home after a good run, he is happy and relaxed. A man is no different.

When my boys were young, I made sure they had time to run, play and unleash all their wild boy energy before dinner. I used to joke and say, "I have to run my dogs so they'll sleep well." Like little animals, they needed to be physically active before they could unwind and behave.

You don't need to run your top dog because he can do it for himself—if you let him. So let him. And make it very clear that it pleases you to see him happy. He'll be better off for it, and so will you.

Let him play basketball with his friends, partake in a regular tennis game or throw the football around on Sunday afternoons. Let him go for a jog before you saddle him with weekend chores and kid duties. Let him go to the gym with the guys after work. Let him join that rugby, soccer or basketball team. Let him go skiing, rafting or hiking with his buddies. Better still, encourage him to be active any way he likes. You will reap the benefits of his good health and better mood. He will love you for it, just like your dog loves you for taking him to the beach or the park and letting him run freely.

Most of all, let your man know that seeing him happy and healthy makes you happier than having a perfect lawn and a clean garage. If you treat your man like a dog, you will feel the same joy for his exploits as you do when your dog catches a Frisbee in mid-air or runs headlong into the surf to fetch a stick. Even if he gets dirty. Even if he smells. Even if you would rather go to a movie or work on that mile-long to-do list.

When they face death,  men and women rarely wish they had worked harder and longer. Instead, they wish they had played more often and loved more deeply.

# TAKE GOOD CARE OF HIM

*"It is easy to love the people far away.
It is not always easy to love those close to us.
It is easier to give a cup of rice to relieve hunger
than to relieve the loneliness and pain of someone
unloved in our own home.
Bring love into your home, for this is where our
love for each other must start."*
Mother Teresa

You feed your dog, walk him, bathe him, brush him, burn off his ticks, and take him to the vet. You even pick up his poop, at least if you live in a town and want your neighbors to like you. You do numerous tasks to ensure your dog's well-being. They aren't always pleasant or fun, but you do them because you are a responsible dog owner who loves and respects her pet.

Relationships come with responsibilities too, but we often fail to recognize them until it is too late.

## Give your dog a bone

Isn't it great to feed your dog the same thing every day and have him love you for it? He never turns his nose up, just goes straight for the bowl. He's happy to be fed regularly, and even happier when there is a special treat or a juicy bone.

Unless your man is a fussy gourmet, he's probably just as grateful as your dog is to get something to eat when he's hungry. It could be the same meat, potatoes and veggies every night, and he would still be happy. It could be a frozen meal or canned ravioli or a pizza. It's the attitude of love and caring that you bring to a meal that makes it a pleasure, whether you cook it, order it or make it together. (Now I'm not saying the woman should be the cook. That depends on who is better at it and enjoys it more. But if you are the designated cook, add a dash of love.)

Would you say to your dog, "You know, I just don't feel like giving you dinner tonight?" Even if you are dead-tired, you feed him with affection. You would never nag your dog when he's eating, or recite your day's travails, or get angry because he isn't listening to you.

When your dog starts licking his bowl in the evening, you get the dog food and feed him. Your man has to wait until you're good and ready. Unless he is the cook, he would rather get take-out for both of you than feel bad about the meal you feel "forced" to prepare ONCE AGAIN. Do it or don't, but don't make it a chore that ruins everyone's appetite. No one needs to be guilt-tripped about something as rudimentary as eating.

Opening a can of soup is no harder than opening a can of dog food, yet many women feel resentful if it's for a man and happy if it's for a dog. "All I do is cook and clean." "You don't appreciate what I do for you." "I'm not your slave."

Actually, you *are* your dog's slave. He can't open the can himself, or fill the water bowl. He relies on you completely for his most basic needs, and you accept the responsibility with grace and patience.

Your man is your partner, your lover and your friend. At least he should be. He doesn't need you to feed him; he needs you to love him. Like a dog, he is content with a plain, filling meal, whether he makes it or you make it or you both make it. Nothing ruins a relationship faster than resentment and anger, especially when you spoil what could have been a happy, relaxing meal. (Women with small children are allowed the occasional breakdown.)

If you love your man, be at least as uncomplaining and dependable about feeding him as you are about feeding your dog. Then, when you give him that delicious bone as an extra treat, he'll run around in circles for you.

## Show concern for his health

The minute your precious dog limps, looks sick or gets hurt, you rush him to the vet for treatment. He doesn't even have to ask. When your husband gets sick, you ignore him or encourage him to "buck up" or tell him what he's feeling is nothing compared with child-birth. Instead of helping him get better and encouraging him to see a doctor, you make him feel worse by belittling his pain, some-times with regrettable results.

Women love to complain that their men are "such babies." They exchange humorous anec-dotes and ignore their men, who may already view seeing a doctor as somewhat unmanly. So, the wife tells her husband who has recur-ring pains in his chest that he just eats too much and has heartburn—until he suffers a heart attack.

That would never happen to your dog. You pay attention to his every move and attend to him with love when he is sick. You administer medicines and preventive treat-ments. You care.

"But I do care for my man, I really do." In your mind you may care, but thoughts don't always generate meaningful actions. Many women behave as if they didn't care at all.

Next time your husband has a fever or the flu or a broken arm, act as if he is your favorite dog, not a pain in the ass. (But beware of acting like his mother — that's almost worse in the long run.)

## Don't overfeed him

What about the touchy subject of weight? As more and more Americans become obese and then sick, you have to wonder who is killing whom. My Serbian grandmother used to say "eat honey, eat" to my grandfather with an evil-sounding chuckle that said it all. Eat yourself to death if that's what you want. It made him control himself, at least some of the time.

When you see a seriously overweight dog, you think to yourself, "What kind of neurotic uncaring person would let their dog get so fat?" And when the vet says your dog needs to lose a few pounds, you buy low-fat kibble and feed him less. After all, you want your dog to stick around as long as possible. I even know women who grind raw meat and mix it with rice and vegetables because they want their dogs to have the best. (Fast food is good enough for their men.)

At the risk of being regarded as traditional (which I am definitely not!), I will state the obvious: in many households, it is the woman who buys the food most of the time. Therefore, if a man is overweight it is partly because of the food his wife brings into the home. Or because of the healthy food she fails to bring home, which leads him to eat fast food every night. Of course, in those cases both of them will probably be unhealthy. The family dog may outlive them.

Now, if you learn to treat your man like a dog you adore, you will do everything possible to keep him healthy. You will heed the doctor's advice to lose weight. You will select different food, get rid of junk food, and prepare healthy meals. And you will make the man who should be your top dog walk or run with you every day until he is as healthy and sleek as a beautiful Greyhound.

## Keep his bed warm and his beer cold

At my house, Rocky always has a warm place to sleep, whether it's on my bed, on a chair or in his doggie bed. His bowl is full of clean water. His toys are nearby and the door to the yard is open.

Dogs are satisfied with simple pleasures, and so are men. They deserve a comfortable home where they can relax and do what they like without being scolded or scared. They should be able to kick off their shoes and enjoy a beer or sit in their favorite old lazy boy (which you would love to get rid of but don't because you know better). Your man shouldn't have to fight for personal space or cherished possessions because you decide the den should be neat and pretty and the coffee table free of feet.

Men shouldn't be made to feel like unwanted male guests in a female dictator-ship, yet they often do. Think of it this way: would you banish your wonderful dog to the yard and never let him curl up next to you, stinky breath and all? Or would you let him be the dog he is and accept that dirty paws and stinky breath are a small price to pay for love, loyalty and companionship? Would you wash his bed every day when you know he prefers it to smell like dog, not detergent? Would you take away his favorite plush toy because it didn't match the carpet?

Why deny men or dogs the privilege to enjoy what they enjoy?

## Don't be neurotic about cleaning

A man doesn't want to live in a showcase home; he wants to live in a real place where he can be himself. It is often the woman who forces herself to keep an immaculate house, then frets and stresses if anything is out of place. Your man would prefer that you be less neurotic and more loving. He will never notice a little dust on the mantel, but he will notice when you act angry and crazy about cleanliness.

A spotless house means nothing to a dog either; in fact, the vacuum cleaner alarms him. Your dog teaches you to relax by spending time with him instead of wasting time with over-zealous housework. If you can relax for your dog, why can't you relax for your man? You'll be taking care of his need for comfort and freedom, not your need for perfection and control.

I confess that I am a neat freak who can become physically distressed at the sight of dirt or disorder. My obsession with stainless steel is especially ridiculous, leading to hours of pointless polishing of stove, dishwasher and refrigerator. Instead of curling up in bed with someone who prefers me to shiny appliances, I will often stay up late cleaning and re-cleaning stubborn streaks and smudges as

if their eradication were a path to enlighten-
ment. I tell people it soothes me when all it
really does is reinforce a neurotic need for
perfection and a reaction of despair when it
cannot be achieved.

After years of meaningless cleaning, I still
need to remind myself every day that my
compulsion for order is unhealthy, unproduc-
tive and doomed to fail. My challenge, and
perhaps yours as well, is to transcend empty
routines that make everyone else uptight.
Bringing love into your home means bringing love to beings, not things.

## TELL HIM WHAT YOU WANT,
## BUT DON'T TALK HIM TO DEATH

*"You've got to ask! Asking is, in my opinion,
the world's most powerful — and neglected — secret
to success and happiness."*
Percy Ross

It is an undisputed fact that women talk much more than men do. It is also known that they say less about what they really want and more about everything else.

Except with their dogs, if they are dog lovers (which I assume anyone reading this book must be). You know your dog can't read your mind, so you tell him in a few words what you expect from him. If he is a well-trained, intelligent dog, he will soon anticipate what you want with just a little cue—an upturned palm, perhaps, or familiar words such as walk, leash or park.

## Talk is overrated

Imagine how confused your dog would be if you expected him to listen to a barrage of words and guess what you wanted from him. And how alarmed he would be if you got angry because "he just didn't get it." You can talk all day to your dog, but you don't expect him to listen. You don't even expect him to bark or whimper in agreement.

Like dogs, men appreciate honesty and directness. You can't expect them to catch every complicated nuance and extract a meaning from it. Men want to solve problems, not listen to them in minute detail, the way women would prefer them to, just for the sake of listening.

When you go on and on about your day and who did what horrible thing to you and how that felt and did he hear that your best friend's mother is in the hospital and, by the way, you are thinking of quitting your job because your boss is a jerk, a man will wonder if you are asking him to fix something or just getting on his nerves with too many details. If he zones out, you are sure to catch him and accuse him of never listening to you. If he offers a solution, you will tell him he doesn't understand.

What to do? If you treat him like a wonderful dog, you will try to be clear, direct and loving. You will not expect him to be your girlfriend. You will leave him alone when he's chilling out after a long day at work. You will kiss him, hold his hand and rub his shoulders. You will greet him with enthusiasm when you or he gets home and let him know that you missed him by hugging him instead of attacking him with words. Your dog-man will respond with love and relief.

Our dogs don't talk at all, yet they can be our best companions and teachers, imparting wisdom through their actions and through their joy in being. Likewise, silence can add intensity to a relationship, creating a bond unsullied by the damage hurtful words often leave in their wake. Value the silence between you and your man. It does not have to be filled, only savored.

## Silence is golden

Nothing calms me more than sitting in complete silence with Rocky next to me, whether it's on the sofa, at the beach or in the backyard. I started experimenting with my partner, sitting quietly next to him in the car or on the sofa and trying to get past the awkwardness of no conversation.

At first, he asked me if I was all right. My usual impulse is to ask questions and expect answers, or tell a little anecdote about someone we both know, or say something witty to make him laugh. Instead, I bit my tongue and said nothing.

Gradually, something in the silence shifted from anxious and weird to peaceful and intimate. Not feeling that I had to talk was a letting go of expectations. For him, not feeling that he had to listen and respond was an immense relief. Now, sitting quietly together seems natural and comfortable.

Dogs are content to be near you while you go about your day. You can make phone calls, pay bills, sit at your computer or vacuum the living room. (Just kidding about the vacuum… it drives some dogs crazy.) If they can hear you or see you, their need for companionship is being met, and because they are pack animals, companionship is essential.

I don't think it's too much of a stretch to suggest that men, as pack animals, also crave companionship. And that companionship doesn't require you to entertain them, talk constantly or pause to ask them a question or two or ten. Being around you is satisfying enough in itself, and being around you comfortably and quietly is nirvana.

I still talk too much, but at least I have learned how to shut up on occasion. Who says an old dog lover can't learn new tricks?

## Tell it like it is

Both dogs and men like to know what's expected of them. They prefer consistency. Will you act happy one day and mad the next for no reason? Will certain actions be rewarded every time with love, praise or gratefulness?

Men are happiest when they don't have to read your mind or guess what you want them to do. You are straightforward and honest with your dog. Why not with your man?

How happy most men would be if we gave them directions. When he wonders what you want for your birthday, you could say, "I really love the pearl earrings in the second case by the side door at Macys." Bingo, problem solved. Or, "For our anniversary I was thinking we could go to that little hotel we loved so much in the Napa Valley." Then offer to make the arrangements. What a relief for him.

It's the rare man who can guess what you want, in or out of bed. Why does a typical woman say, "I'll be happy with whatever gift you choose," when her man is desperately seeking clues? Then he buys her a blender and she cries.

I remember one awful anniversary when my ex-husband gave me new exercise clothes. Unfortunately, it was two weeks after I had a baby… What prompted the gift was probably a poor-little-me remark about how awful I looked and how I wondered if I would ever get my figure back. He meant well, I'm sure of it now, but at the time the gift unleashed a cascade of tears and self-pity that lasted a good three days. I should have asked for a bracelet, or even a blender.

The younger generation has gotten savvier with the gift problem. I would never have dared ask for money for my birthday, yet my boyfriend's daughter and her friends have no qualms about it. Their husbands are ever so grateful to be spared the agony of shopping.

I, on the other hand, still cling to the romantic notion that a gift a man chooses for you means more than money—especially a gift you have coveted and somehow led him to buy for you. That sounds hypocritical, and it probably is, but I don't care.

My justification is that if he were your dog, he'd know exactly what you wanted, because you would show him, with or without words. I believe this theory encompasses far more than gift-giving and is almost fail-proof.

Let's say you are unhappy because your dog growls at another dog; you cue him right away according to how you have trained him. He stops, and that's that. But if you are unhappy because your husband flirts with a woman you hate (I know, I know, "hate" is a very strong word!), you stew about it for a week or two and mutter snide remarks you hope will make him feel bad. They never do, because half the time he's not sure what the hell you're mad about.

If you want your man to accompany you to the supermarket, you beat around the bush and try to manipulate him into feeling guilty enough to come with you. If you want your dog to get in the car, you say, "Come on, let's go for a ride."

If you are dying to go out for dinner, you complain about how sick you are of cooking and how tedious your life is. Your man tunes you out. If you said, "You know, there's this new restaurant I want to try. I made reservations for tomorrow night," he would pay attention and either answer, "Great idea," or "I can't do it tomorrow. How about Saturday?"

We like to say that men are clueless when the truth is that we rarely give them enough clues. If you treat your man like a dog, you won't expect him to guess what you want and when you want it—not even a trained psychologist could. Instead, you tell him in twenty words or less and praise him when he gets it right. His anxiety level will drop and so will yours.

And if he gets it wrong anyway, don't cling to the disappointment and bring it up every time you have a fight. For instance, if you tell him again and again that you love lilacs, and for Valentine's Day, he buys you carnations, flowers you despise, you don't rush away crying and from then on repeat, "Remember that awful Valentine's Day when you brought me those horrible red carnations even though you should have known how much I hate them because they remind me of funerals? I think you did it on purpose." Of course he didn't do it on purpose! He just wasn't listening when you gave your "carnations and funerals" speech. And even if he brings you lilacs for the next twenty years, you still won't let him forget. (And soon he'll associate Valentine's Day with a funeral.)

Of course, if you are a smart woman, you'll just smile and say thank you. Next year, you'll leave a big note on the bathroom mirror that says, "I love lilacs! I HATE carnations!"

As for the "in bed" part, every woman's magazine stresses the importance of letting a man know what you like, without embarrassment or coyness. He won't get hints and he won't notice what you think are obvious clues. So go on and say it, or you will be doomed to repetitive lovemaking that he assumes you enjoy because you never speak up.

Replace manipulation, dishonesty, avoidance and all those other phony tricks with clear communication and tenacious devotion. Your relationship can only improve.

## ABOVE ALL, BE KIND

---

*"The highest form of wisdom is kindness."*
The Talmud

Dog owners often say that their dog brings out the best in them. If you spend any time with dog lovers, you cannot help but notice how kind and caring they are to their cherished pets. They are gentle and loving to their animals, without being so indulgent as to endanger their lives with bad food or inconsistent discipline.

When your dog brings you your slippers or fends off raccoons or startles a would-be burglar, you are grateful and full of praise. You reward him with kind words, petting and sweet talk. You don't mind if the slippers are soggy and his barking wakes up the neighbors. He is your hero.

You man will fix a broken chair, power wash the house and build shelves in the closet, and the whole time you will chide him for not being expert enough, or careful enough, to do a good job. He'll surprise you with breakfast in bed, and instead of appreciating his thought-fulness, you will criticize his cooking. He is not your hero. If you treat him like an incompetent loser, he will begin to feel like one.

Perhaps you are a stay-at-home-mom, and every day your husband goes to a job he doesn't particularly like so you and your chil-dren can live well. He does it because he loves you, and he should be your hero. Yet most of the time you don't even acknowledge his effort let alone thank him with kindness and affec-tion or feel compassion for him or treat him with dignity and respect. You are not happy, and neither is he.

When your dog is dutiful, you notice and respond. Your dog is happy because you are happy with him. Most men are dutiful every day, whether at work or at home, whether they feel like it or not, and no one notices let alone thanks them and makes them feel proud. If their women are constantly unhappy, men are unhappy too. The negativity grinds them down and strips them of feeling—they resem-ble listless, unresponsive dogs that have been in the pound too long.

Mark is an example. A good-looking man, he seems beat down by his partner's inexpli-cable anger and nagging. "Sue's always mad at me," he says. "I think I've done something to please her, and the next minute, she finds fault with it, and me. I'm ready to give up." Instead of thanking Mark for putting in a door to her new guest unit, Elizabeth became unhinged when she discovered that her cable wire had been cut. She blamed Mark for the misdeed, even though he hadn't gone near it. "I've had it," he says. "She treats me like an idiot no matter what I do."

If kindness is the highest form of wisdom, then both men and women spend most of their lives in stupidity. It starts in their relationships and spreads like waves of negative energy into their communities, their workplaces, their governments and, ultimately, their earth. The result is a pall of greed, hatred, aggression, prejudice and selfishness that pollutes the beauty and purity of life as it might be were we all more enlightened.

## Practicing kindness

We are capable of so much more, and it begins at home, in the way we treat each other. If you have the capacity to love and nurture your dog with kindness and devotion, surely that capacity does not vanish when you turn your attention to your significant other. If we can be kind and gentle some of the time, we can be kind and gentle much more of the time than we think.

To wake up to this realization and change your behavior, think about what makes you so willing to be kind to your dog, even when you feel lousy. With your dog, only the present moment counts. You are engaged right then and there, with no baggage from the past and no anxiety about the future. Your dog takes you out of yourself and your petty fears and concerns and anchors you to the present. A dog's very nature of trust and love and immediate feedback helps you transcend whatever reality you are trapped in. You accept that moment of interaction completely and lovingly. It is what it is, and it makes you calm and happy.

With your man, it is hard to feel that bond of engagement without the intrusion of unforgiving thoughts, noxious habits, limiting perceptions and past or present misunderstandings. If you treated your man like your dog, you would be "right here, right now," linked in present love and awareness. It would be a clear connection, not one buzzing with resentful interference and negative anticipation.

Most women I know are not kind to themselves, either. They engage in constant negative self-talk, such as "I am fat and ugly," "I am such a loser," "I am a bad mother," "I am so un-together and the other moms are perfect," "I have wasted my life," and so on. You would never say those things to someone else because they are cruel, yet you say them to yourself. That kind of cruelty mixed with the guilt and anxiety so many women fall prey to will eventually infect how you deal with others, especially your partner.

Kindness begins inside our hearts and minds, in loving ourselves and forgiving ourselves, in  replacing negative self-talk with gentle appreciation and positive emotions. By practicing kindness, remembering kindness, being kindness, perhaps we can achieve the same easy rapport with our men as we do with our dogs. We put away self-criticism when we are with our dogs because they adore us and fill us with confidence and love. This inward shift from judgment to compassion is a first step in the practice of kindness.

Kindness is a difficult practice, a daily program of self-awareness. The love we have for our dogs and for ourselves when we are with them can be a gentle reminder of the importance of kindness and compassion in the world, starting with how we treat our loved ones.

## A true love story

One of the kindest men I know takes his shaggy Collie-mix to the same dog park I frequent. When I first started going there, I would often see Kurt sitting in contemplation on a bench facing west. As I got to know him better, he told me a remarkable story of love and devotion and loss, one that epitomizes the ideal of kindness and loyalty in a marriage.

Kurt and Sheryl were married for more than twenty years. He is a much-lauded calligrapher and she was a graphic artist. They often collaborated on projects and shared a love of travel, Italian food, environmental politics and, of course, dogs. Sheryl, Kurt told me, was a passionate woman with a big heart and a larger-than-life personality. He was quiet, while she was outgoing with charisma to spare.

A strong believer in alternative medicine, Sheryl refused to go to the doctor when she started having stomach problems, then "plumbing" problems. "I should have forced her to go," says Kurt, "but she was stubborn and completely convinced that she was doing the right thing. I was used to letting her have things her way."

When the pain became unbearable, she finally relented. It was colon cancer in an aggressive, advanced form that had become inoperable. They took one last trip to Italy, but all too soon, Sheryl was bedridden and in constant pain. Kurt took care of her himself, day and night, administering her morphine, feeding her, reading to her and making sure she was as comfortable as possible.

As the cancer spread to her brain, Sheryl became irrational, delusional and sometimes downright mean. At one point, she became convinced that Kurt was trying to steal her money and property and insisted on sleeping in the living room. Kurt and Sheryl didn't even own their home, let alone stocks or savings, but he waited patiently for her to come around, continuing to care for her with tenderness and compassion until she begrudgingly agreed to come back to the bedroom. He laughs at the memory, and tells other tales of her feistiness and passion, all with tender gratitude for what he had and no hint of self-pity for what he lost.

"Nothing I have done in my life means more to me than taking care of my wife when she was dying," he says. "It was the deepest, most loving experience a man can have. I wouldn't trade it for anything."

That experience has made Kurt conscious of suffering wherever he sees it. He feels for the aging dog that limps, or struggles to walk on shaky legs, or bravely chases a ball with no hope of catching it at all. He leaves every person he talks to with a touch of his calm kindness…and he doesn't even know it.

A friend told me Kurt had dedicated a bench to his wife, the bench where he often sits alone. When I first wandered up the little rise to see it, I was moved to tears. Above her name he had carved in beautiful script: "Artist, Environmentalist, Sweetheart." And beneath the inscription, "Love, forever."

Whenever I am feeling cynical or angry, unloving or negative, I sit on Sheryl's bench in the evening, with Rocky and his friends playing joyfully around me, and look to the distant hills where the sun sets in swirls of gray and gold. There, I am filled with the peaceful certitude that true love and compassion do indeed exist. Sheryl's bench is a healing place that exudes the energy of loving kindness to all who seek its solace.

## Yes, we can change

If we are to be truly fulfilled in our lives, we cannot live in constant anger and misunderstanding, intent on a future that we think will be better but that will inevitably be an even more damaged version of a life lived without kindness. A bad relationship today will be a worse one tomorrow if we don't change.

Dog lovers understand the sense of connection and love that needs no words yet is so deeply felt. If we are capable of that connection with an animal, we are capable of having it with any human being we love. And from there, we are capable of feeling a connection with all beings sharing life on this planet.

It all begins with the practice of kindness. How does your man feel when he is with you? Is he proud and happy and fulfilled? Are you as loving with him as you are with your dog?

Living with and loving dogs can open our hearts to the kindness that is already there, the kindness we bestow without effort or guile. Let your dog bring out the best in you. That is, the kind, loving, happy, playful, patient, loyal, grateful, friendly, attentive, protective, forgiving, engaged, centered, undemanding, affectionate, unselfconscious you — the woman who loves her dog and can love her man just as fully.

## RELATIONSHIP WISDOM FROM THE TAO OF DOG

*"Until one has loved an animal,
a part of one's soul remains unawakened."*
Anatole France

If you have decided you want to change and be a kinder, more loving person to your partner, you need look no further than your furry soul mate for guidance. Sure, you may now realize that you act like two different women depending on whether you are with your man or your dog, but how do you teach yourself to be the person your dog thinks you are, now and forever?

Maybe you've finally awakened to the fact that you are not giving enough love—maybe you've even examined it—but how do you change your negative habits and patterns of behavior? How do you attain a higher spiritual plane that will transform your relationship? Follow the Tao of Dog and you will be on the right path.

## Happiness is a natural state of being

We often think that happiness is a fluke, something that only a lucky few experience, something that will come to us if we are fortunate or if we work hard enough or if we make all the "right" choices. Yet your dog shows you every day that happiness is a natural state of being. It is we who obscure it or banish it through our blindness and negativity. And in our relationships, it is we who focus on the bad and think away the happiness we deserve.

As I was driving Rocky to the park one day, he was sticking his curly-haired head out the window and singing a little song of happiness. Well, that's how I interpreted it. My boyfriend said Rocky was whining and it was annoying. "Should I tell him his happiness is bugging us?" I asked. Rocky was just being a dog, happy to be alive and relishing his outing to the utmost.

Happy people often annoy unhappy people. So what. Let unhappy people be the losers, not you. By recognizing that happiness is there for the taking even when "bad" things are happening, you can change your personal vibration and attract more of it. Who hasn't met people beset by injury, sickness or tragedy who nevertheless spread a glow of harmony and love? And who hasn't had encounters with people who suck away the positive energy around them with their complaints, self-pity, anger and selfishness? Attitude is everything.

Dogs add positive energy to the world. I know a dog who lost her front left leg in a car accident yet cheerfully carries on, oblivious to her rather pitiful appearance and not at all discouraged by her awkwardness and frequent stumbles. Happiness is Betsy's natural state of being, and nothing can change that. She has accepted change and moved on, happy to celebrate life as it is now.

Even my friend Alex's gentle pitbull, Bulla, when struggling to get up on aging arthritic hips, will wag his tail in joy just for a hug or a biscuit. He is in pain, but that does not obliterate his happiness. He still looks as if he's smiling.

Instead of asking what's wrong with your partner or your marriage, ask yourself what's right and hold optimism in your heart. Like attracts like. If you go around moaning and groaning about your relationship, you will have more and more to moan and groan about. If, instead, you focus your thoughts and actions on what makes you happy, you will have more and more to celebrate.

Let your dog be your guru of happiness. When you start feeling negative or think a bad thought about your partner, stop and look at your dog. Use him as a cue to replace a harmful inner judgment with a positive thought or memory. By breathing in and absorbing the happiness of your dog, you can create your own practice of positive thinking. It may be impossible to change someone else, but it is very possible — and very important — to change the way you see the world.

## Rest and relaxation are essential

Rocky spends a lot of his day lying in the sun, snuggling on the sofa or sleeping in his little bed. He instinctively knows how to take care of himself. But do we women? The busier our lives get, the less time we take for ourselves. Our reservoir of calm and well-being is usually empty, which means we struggle to nurture others and fail to nurture ourselves. Bitterness grows in our hearts, our thoughts turn to complaints and resentments, and soon all that negativity is speeding back toward us in the form of sickness, anger, fatigue and depression.

Maybe we can't plop down any time we want to take a little nap, but we can structure our day so that a bit of it is reserved just for us. It could be a jog, a hot bath or lunch with a friend. It could be a glass of wine shared with our partner before dinner. It could be sleeping in on a Sunday or a girls' night out. Whatever it is, it must take us away from work and duty, worry and sacrifice.

You cannot improve your relationship if you don't have a good relationship with yourself. If you dislike yourself, deny yourself, martyr yourself or abuse yourself, the repercussions are all negative. How can you cherish others when you are mean to yourself? Without a strong, confident "me," there can be no solid, happy "us." Your relationship with your man will tend to mimic your relationship with yourself — and that could be very sad.

Each time you see your dog stretch out, belly up, paws batting the air in glee, think, "Have I done something relaxing today?" "Have I recharged my batteries and nourished my soul?" Then make it a habit to do something just for you every single day. That way, when you are with your man, you won't be resenting that he has more fun, more time or more freedom than you do. You won't be so exhausted that you create distance from him instead of closeness. You'll be giving him love because you feel as good as he does.

## Less is often more

By watching your dog, you realize that doing nothing does not necessarily equate to accomplishing nothing. Sitting still, breathing deeply, absorbing nature through all of your senses are activities that make you calm, receptive and loving. They open your heart and silence the meaningless chatter in your head. You become peaceful, grounded in the present where kindness and love can manifest.

Dogs know how to sit quietly and observe the world around them. We rush around creating stress for ourselves, blind to the beauty of the life around us. By observing the Tao of Dog, we can learn to slow down and stay for a moment. In stillness we can rediscover ourselves.

Too much talking can also obscure what is really important. Saying nothing can be a healing tool in a relationship. Instead of talking, try listening for a change. Talk less and listen more and your communication will improve. Women say men don't listen to them. Maybe it's because we say way too much for them to take in. Have you ever thought that your man doesn't feel that you listen to him? I know many men who give up trying to get a word in edgewise. They feel that their women dismiss their feelings and fail to hear them when they try to communicate what matters to them.

Communicating with touch, like your dog does, is a very simple way to do less and accomplish more. Studies have shown that couples who kiss and touch for no reason many times a day are less prone to stress and depression. Touch releases feel-good brain chemicals and leaves you physically and emotionally stronger and more connected—better able to cope with life's difficulties together.

## The present is all there is

No person I know lives in the present as intensely as my dog does. When we get to the dog park, Rocky shoots out of the car and runs to see who is there, what is happening. Then he will race back and greet me with exuberant affection as if he hadn't seen me two minutes ago. He will repeat this again and again, never tiring of showing his joy and appreciation.

If we could learn from our dogs to be positive and present in every moment we share with our men, we would eliminate so much confusion, misunderstanding and conflict. Instead of telling them hours later that our feelings were hurt by blah blah blah, we would take each moment as a chance to be loving and honest and stop ourselves from relationship sabotage. We would realize we have a choice in how we react, and that choice is made in the moment. Perhaps we would realize in that moment that a hurtful word can pierce a tender heart and leave it wounded forever after.

By the amount of time we spend rehashing the past and wishing for the future, it would appear that we are unable to comprehend the all-encompassing reality of the present. Everything occurs right now, and the more we embrace the present, the better our future will be. The actions and thoughts we have today create the world we will live in tomorrow.

Accepting our relationships in the moment and nourishing them with loving thoughts and actions help us create a beautiful future for ourselves.

One powerful foe of loving in the moment is our need to be right. A dog doesn't care if he is right or wrong. He has nothing to prove. But we women get completely distraught if our man doesn't agree with us or doesn't recognize our expertise or doesn't want to back down in an argument.

If you lived in the present moment, you would recognize most arguments for what they are: foolish displays of ego that waste precious time and leave ill feelings and lingering resentments in their wake. If you squelch an argument before it explodes, you are freeing yourself to enjoy the present. By not resisting, you preclude anger from arising and allow the present to unfold naturally.

Easier said than done, I know. But the Tao of Dog emphasizes conserving energy for joy and not caring who is right or wrong, only who is happy in the moment. That is not to say that we can always avoid conflict, just that it need not be a battle that determines how much love we withhold, and how much pain we create for each other.

Being present in a conflict means sticking to the issue at hand, not using it to launch a deadly attack full of past resentments and future grenades. It means being honest about our flaws and being understanding of our men's. It requires cultivating calm and patience so we can connect lovingly to our partners— and connection can only occur in the absence of aggression and prejudice.

## Welcome every day with joy

When Rocky senses that I am awake, he comes to the side of the bed, puts his black paws on the mattress and looks at me with big brown eyes that say, "Come on, hurry up, it's a beautiful day and there's so much to do." He then starts to lick and lick and lick until I roll out of bed, shower and get dressed — while he sits shaking his curly-cue tail to urge me on.

Our morning walk is always the same, but to Rocky it is always new. New places to stop, new corners to sniff, new critters to chase. His enthusiasm is boundless; everything seems new because he is not repeating a routine walk. He is living this particular walk, open to whatever it will bring, without any preconceptions or judgments to block his enjoyment and discovery. He runs back and forth, sniffing everything, darting up hills, greeting his dog friends with a happy bark and kicking up the dirt with his back legs in a triumphant display of male confidence. In other words, he experiences perfect freedom.

And what do you do when you take the obligatory morning walk? Chances are, you are locked in a mind full of problems and complaints, plots and plans. You are writing a grocery list or mulling over something your man did that bugged you. You do not see that the daffodils have bloomed, that a fat robin pecks at the bright green grass, that the sun has made a million rainbows on every dewdrop on every leaf. You do not hear a thousand trilling birds or the wind singing in the treetops. You do not feel the pure bliss of being alive even though your dog is right there showing you the way. You have become blind and tired and dead to the world as you trudge alone imprisoned by your ego and alienated from your true self.

And when you get home, do you see a living, breathing, loving man? Or do you see whatever toxic judgments, bad memories, regrets and failures your mind has superimposed on him?

If we could observe and anticipate the good things about being alive each day, no matter how familiar or tedious they seem, we would bring joy to those we love and happiness to ourselves. Instead of putting out gloom and doom before the day has yet begun, we would be projecting happiness and therefore attracting it on every level to ourselves and our loved ones. Our energy would be transformed and, left to work its magic, would change our reality from bad to good all day long.

Watch your dog and how he transmutes the humdrum into excitement and delight. Observe how this affects you. Does your dog leave you feeling energized and loved? How do you leave your man feeling? Think about it and tune your energy into your dog's every morning. Imitate his enthusiastic way of treating people, especially with your partner. By aligning with a positive being you will bring good energy to your man and leave him feeling happy to be sharing his life with you.

## Be grateful for the little things

No woman I know thinks she has enough of anything: clothes, shoes, time, love, space, attention, jewelry, furniture, vacations or whatever else she craves. We focus so much on what we don't have that we fail to be grateful for what we do have.

Not so our canine friends. Dogs are grateful for the smallest favor: a sweet voice, a short scratch, a leftover tidbit of meat, a daily walk down the same path. They know how to rejoice for others: if you are happy, your dog is happy too. Dogs know how to celebrate all the little events they are grateful for, because to them life is one continuous celebration. You cannot help but be grateful if you value and embrace every moment of life.

Practicing gratitude may be the platitude of our time; perhaps that's because we need the lesson so much. Be grateful to your partner the way your dog is grateful to have you in his life: by showing affection and appreciation spontaneously, effortlessly and enthusiastically.

It's so easy to attack your man when he does something you think is wrong, mean, selfish or careless. To initiate gratefulness in your relationship, make it a point to compliment your partner when he does something you like.

A compliment is much more powerful than an insult. A recrimination puts your man on the defensive and goads him to counterattack when the occasion arises, as it inevitably will. Negativity has now been squared and squared again, and will soon become exponential; it will permeate everything you do together until one of you breaks the stalemate with an apology or a kind gesture. A simple thank you for a favor done or a sweet comment will have the opposite effect of dispelling negative vibes and bringing more love your way.

Don't wait for a big gift or a major accomplishment to show your appreciation. Just as a dog shows thanks for any small gesture, learn to say thank you at least once a day for the little things your man does to make you happy.

## Loyalty matters

It seems as if loyalty has become a virtue of the past. The Ancients exalted loyalty and wrote tragedies illustrating the awful events caused by betrayal and faithlessness. But many people today no longer value loyalty, not even loyalty to their families, let alone to their spouses. In this age of casual divorce and careless affairs, we should heed the simplest lesson of all from the Tao of Dog: loyalty is at the core of a loving relationship.

Loyalty in a relationship means fidelity, and fidelity depends on trust. You cannot find a better teacher of fidelity than the dog. Throughout history, he has been the best friend to men and women, the one friend you can depend on no matter what happens. Fido is not called Fido in vain.

Stories abound of dogs who save their masters under the most dangerous conditions; dogs who travel miles and miles to reunite with their families; dogs like the mythical Argus who wait in misery and hunger for their Ulysses to return.

If we cannot share complete trust with our partners, our relationships will be shallow and unfulfilling. Fear and jealousy will gnaw at us, subverting love and innocence. And once we've been betrayed, it is so hard to trust again.

Even when betrayed, women have often been emotionally rescued by the loyalty of their dogs—the kind of loyalty they failed to find in their husbands. Dogs tune in to unhappiness and fear and try to alleviate pain in the humans they love.

When my husband walked out on me and our five children, my despair was deepened when he took our Boxer, Tiny. Even though I had given him Tiny for his birthday six years earlier, she was the family dog. Tiny would find me when I was crying and lie with her head on my lap. She would lick my tears and walk for miles with me. She was better than a therapist or a girlfriend because she asked nothing of me and gave me all her love and attention.

That ended when he moved out and took Tiny with him. After all, he declared, she was his dog. Bereft of dog comfort, I sank deeper and deeper into depression, unable to move or talk or do anything more than the bare mini-mum for my children. I saw no reason to walk without a dog and soon became a recluse.

One day, forced to stop at my husband's office to beg for money, I went hysterical when I saw Tiny on his back porch. My husband said I was embarrassing him and threatened to call the police if I didn't get off his "property." Horrified and humiliated, I ended up huddled in a doorway three blocks away, where I sat crying in the cold, my head folded in shame so no one would recognize me.

Suddenly, I felt a warm tongue on my cheek. Tiny had come to find me. I put my arms around her, and we stayed entwined for at least an hour, until I felt strong enough to walk her back to the office and leave as quietly as possible. Unlike my husband, who found my tears "disgusting" and told me to "pull myself together," Tiny sensed my despair and comforted me as only a loyal dog can. Tiny was being a dog-Buddha in her compassionate determination to ease my suffering.

Observe the unwavering loyalty of your dog and emulate it. And when you sense sadness in your man, comfort him without questioning or lecturing. The loving loyalty you nurture as a couple will keep you together for as long as you live.

## Too much love is impossible

A dog never wastes a chance to show affection. He will give the most love to its owner yet have tons left over to greet a stranger, comfort someone in pain or cure the loneliness of an elder, at least for a while. That's why dogs make such good healers and helpers in hospitals, old age homes and prisons. To them, love is a fountain that keeps on flowing.

People, on the other hand, tend to hoard love and measure it out in teaspoons to those they deem deserving. They are so afraid of being vulnerable, of being hurt, that they withhold love to protect themselves. They don't know that love is the essence of life, that it is their highest calling. Watch your dog and you will see that he holds this knowledge in every moment.

I have seen grown men talk in a baby voice to their dogs and roll around on the ground wrestling and playing with them. These men feel safe opening their love reservoir to their pets because they are not afraid of being judged, mocked or rejected. Just think if your man felt that safe with you! A veil of love and happiness would envelop you all the time.

For dogs, pleasing others is not a chore. It is rewarding in itself. It is what they do without thinking. They are not calculating what they will get in return or feeling obliged to please. They live to please. Maybe that's why we women who love dogs try to please them, too. Their energy becomes our energy, and the exchange is pure joy. Dogs teach us that pleasing others should be something we want to do, not something we have to do, because in the end we will get back at least as much as we give away.

Loving unconditionally is the most important lesson in the Tao of Dog. If you learn just one thing from your dog, let it be that love means forgiving flaws and celebrating life. Most human beings are not blessed with a dog's innate ability to love unconditionally, but through practice and effort we can all get better and better at love.

Treat your man like your adored dog, and let your adored dog become your guru. Your relationship will improve, and you may even **live happily ever after**.

# BIOGRAPHIES

**Maïa Madden** emigrated from France to the United States when she was a toddler. She holds a Bachelor of Arts degree in Comparative Literature from New College, Florida, and a Master's degree in Journalism from the University of California, Berkeley. She has worked as a writer and editor for various publications, including the *Yoga Journal, AM/PM Guide to Northern California, Gentry Magazine, Penny Express* and multiple editions of the *Epicurean Rendezvous Restaurant Guide.* Her most relevant credential, however, is that she has always loved dogs: Kiss, Miss, Yuki, Sharetha, Sage, Abu, Tiny, Aiko and now, Rocky the rock star. They are her inspiration. Maïa lives in Santa Cruz, California.

**Fred Luskin, Ph.D.**, is the author of *Forgive for Love: The Missing Ingredient for a Healthy and Lasting Relationship* and the director of the Stanford Forgiveness Project in Palo Alto,

California. As one of the world's leading researchers and teachers of forgiveness, he has conducted scientific studies on the healing power of forgiveness and developed a seven-step program to teach couples and other therapists forgiveness skills. He is a senior fellow at the Stanford Center on Conflict and Negotiation and an associate professor at the Institute of Transpersonal Psychology.

**Alicia Dickerson** is a professional photographer residing in Portland, Oregon. She graduated from the University of California, Santa Cruz, and continued her study of photography at the Rocky Mountain School of Photography in Montana. Her portraits are pieces of art that capture the unique inner spirit of each animal and reveal the special connections that exist between people and their pets. She is the proud owner of Maya, an Australian Shepherd mix rescued through the Oregon Humane Society.

CPSIA information can be obtained at www.ICGtesting.com
Printed in the USA
BVOW02s1556170414

350824BV00009B/554/P